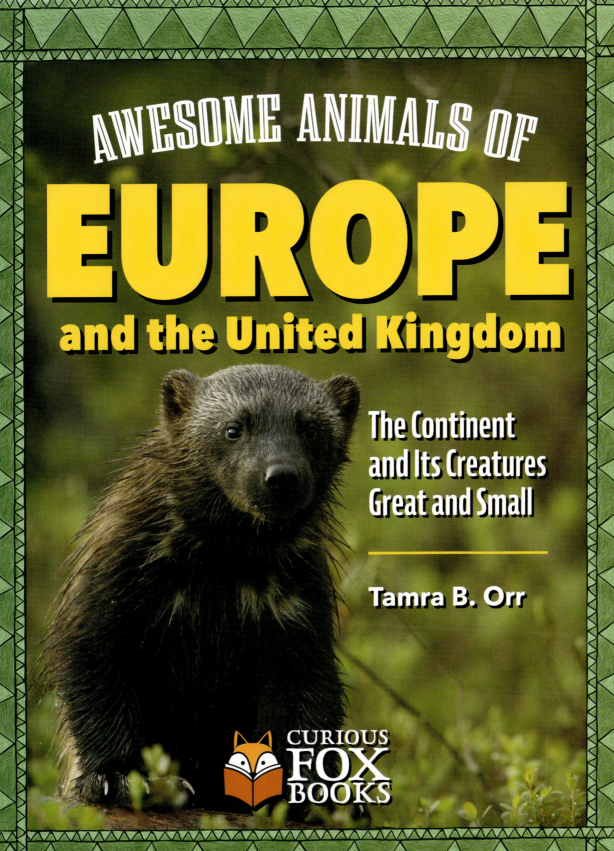

AWESOME ANIMALS OF

EUROPE

and the United Kingdom

The Continent and Its Creatures Great and Small

Tamra B. Orr

CURIOUS FOX BOOKS

Europe is made up of many countries. The largest is Russia. Russia is so large, it's part of both Europe and Asia.

Welcome to Europe! It's made up of many different countries, but it is the second smallest continent.

Europe has all kinds of biomes. In the north, there is the tundra. Little grows here. There are many forests and mountains in Europe. There are also grasslands in the west. Water surrounds Europe on almost every side.

EURASIAN WOLF

Length: 63 inches (160 centimeters), not including tail
Weight: 158 pounds (72 kilograms)
Habitat: mountains, plains, scrublands, and tundra of northern and eastern Europe
Diet: deer, boars, and goats

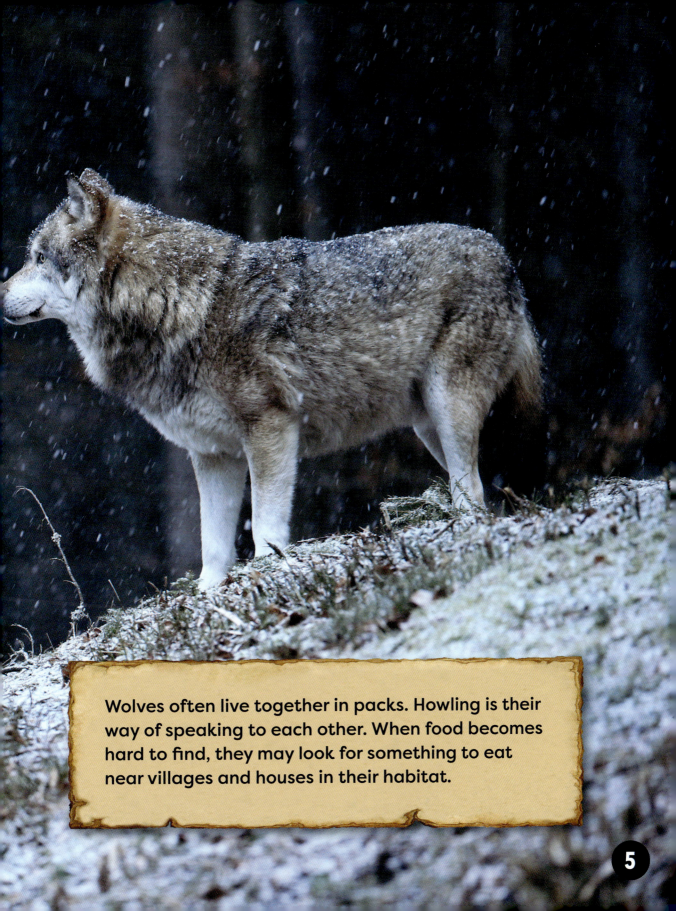

Wolves often live together in packs. Howling is their way of speaking to each other. When food becomes hard to find, they may look for something to eat near villages and houses in their habitat.

Fallow deer are spread throughout Europe, but they are especially found in places like England and Scotland. The fallow deer's white spots are bright during summer but fade away in the winter.

FALLOW DEER

Height: 3 feet (91 centimeters), at shoulders
Weight: 220 pounds (100 kilograms)
Habitat: forests and grasslands of northern, western, and eastern Europe
Diet: grasses, nuts, and fruits

REINDEER

Height: 4 feet (1.2 meters), at shoulders
Weight: 550 pounds (249 kilograms)
Habitat: tundra of Russia and Scandinavia
Diet: grasses, leaves, mosses, and mushrooms

Europe is also home to reindeer. In the winter, they live in the forests; in the spring, they go back to the treeless arctic tundra. They are the only deer in which both males and females have antlers. Reindeer antlers can grow to 53 inches (135 centimeters) long. You might be shorter than a reindeer antler!

Wolverines are small and fierce fighters with powerful jaws and sharp teeth. They can climb trees with their long claws. Wolverines can smell food buried under 20 feet of snow.

WOLVERINE

Length: 51 inches (130 centimeters), including tail
Weight: 66 pounds (30 kilograms)
Habitat: forests and mountains of northern Europe
Diet: small mammals, deer, and sheep

EUROPEAN MINK

Length: 24 inches (61 centimeters), including tail
Weight: 1½ pounds (680 grams)
Habitat: wetlands of Russia, France, and Spain
Diet: frogs, fish, crabs, and insects

The European mink is found near rivers. Its waterproof fur and webbed feet make it a great swimmer as it searches for tasty fish.

While the European mink spends a lot of time in the water, it lives on land. It will sleep for long periods during the winter when it is too cold to leave home. Mink like fish but will also eat frogs, crabs, and even insects.

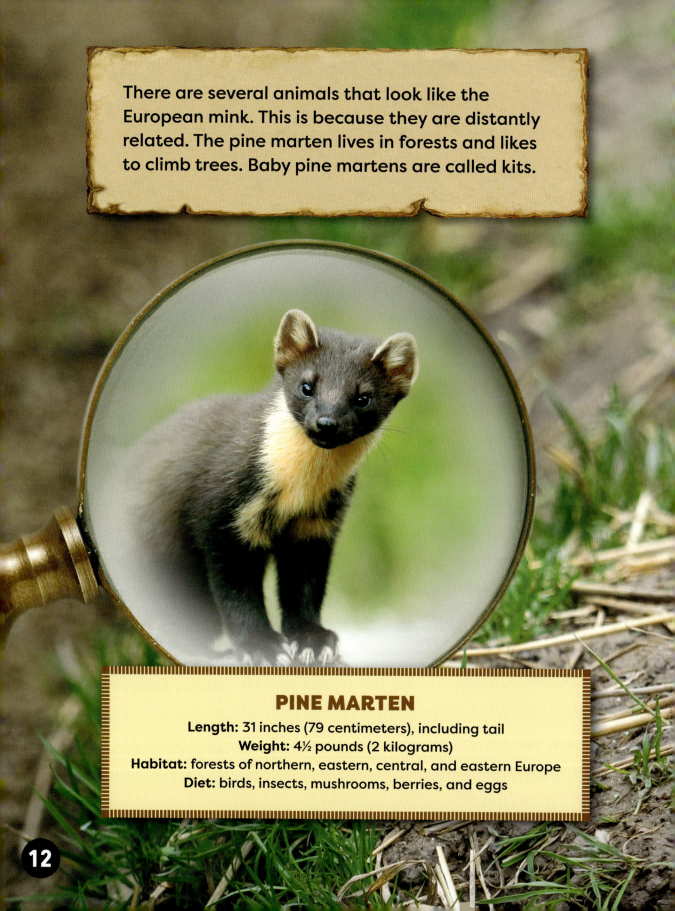

There are several animals that look like the European mink. This is because they are distantly related. The pine marten lives in forests and likes to climb trees. Baby pine martens are called kits.

PINE MARTEN

Length: 31 inches (79 centimeters), including tail
Weight: 4½ pounds (2 kilograms)
Habitat: forests of northern, eastern, central, and eastern Europe
Diet: birds, insects, mushrooms, berries, and eggs

The European polecat lives near rivers, but it does not spend a long time in the water. European polecats are the ancestors of ferrets.

EUROPEAN POLECAT

Length: 29 inches (74 centimeters), including tail
Weight: 3 pounds (1.4 kilograms)
Habitat: wetlands, grasslands, and forests of Europe
Diet: rodents, frogs, birds, and lizards

The European badger has long claws that are perfect for digging holes. Badgers will create large underground homes called setts. These can be as long 328 feet (100 meters) with multiple entrances and rooms. That's almost as long as a football field. Badgers will use straw as bedding. They will clean out old straw before the winter.

EUROPEAN BADGER

Length: 3½ feet (100 centimeters), including tail
Weight: 31 pounds (14 kilograms)
Habitat: grasslands and forests of Europe
Diet: fruits, roots, insects, frogs, and small mammals

COMMON CUCKOO

Wingspan: 24 inches (61 centimeters)
Weight: 4½ ounces (128 grams)
Habitat: grasslands, forests, savannas, and tundra of Europe
Diet: insects

The common cuckoo (**KOO-koo**) gets its name from the call the male bird makes. Cuckoos lay eggs in the nests of other birds. Those other birds will take care of the cuckoo babies after they hatch. In Europe, the sound of the cuckoo means it's spring.

The colorful European goldfinch eats the seeds out of prickly thistles with their sharp, pointed beaks. These birds can often be seen in gardens and parks. When several goldfinches gather together, they are called a charm.

EUROPEAN GOLDFINCH

Wingspan: 10 inches (25 centimeters)
Weight: 2/3 ounce (19 grams)
Habitat: grasslands and forests of Europe
Diet: seeds and insects

The Eurasian brown bear lives in a den, which is a hole dug in the ground or the base of a tree. Baby bears, or cubs, will stay with their moms for about two years. Mother bears are very protective of their young. They will attack any creature that might be threatening their cubs.

EURASIAN BROWN BEAR

Height: 7 feet (2.1 meters), standing
Weight: 780 pounds (354 kilograms)
Habitat: forests, mountains, and tundra of northern Europe
Diet: roots, insects, fish, and large mammals

EUROPEAN HEDGEHOG

Length: 10 inches (25 centimeters)
Weight: 2½ pounds (1.1 kilograms)
Habitat: forests and grasslands of western and northern Europe
Diet: worms, insects, fruits, and mushrooms

The hedgehog will curl up into a ball if it feels scared. There are short but sharp spines on its back for protection. Wild hamsters live in the farmlands of Europe. They store food in their chubby cheeks to eat later. The Norway lemming (**LEM-ing**) starts a great journey every two or three years. Hundreds of them walk together in their quest for food and a new home.

NORWAY LEMMING

Length: 6 inches (15 centimeters)
Weight: 4½ ounces (2 kilograms)
Habitat: mountains, forests, and
tundra of Scandinavia
Diet: grasses and mosses

EUROPEAN HAMSTER

Length: 12 inches (30 centimeters)
Weight: 16 ounces (454 grams)
Habitat: grasslands of eastern Europe
Diet: grasses, seeds, roots, and insects

Europe's tree frog croaks loudly during the day. Tree frogs get hungry at night for insects and can jump very far to catch tasty bugs. They are found in meadows and shrublands across eastern Europe. Tree frogs hibernate during the winter.

EUROPEAN TREE FROG

Length: 1½ inches (3.8 centimeters)
Weight: ⅓ ounce (9 grams)
Habitat: wetlands and forests of western, eastern, and southern Europe
Diet: insects

WELS CATFISH

Length: 9 feet (2.7 meters)
Weight: 440 pounds (200 kilograms)
Habitat: rivers and lakes of eastern and southern Europe
Diet: worms, insects, crabs, birds, fish, and small mammals

The wels (WELLZ) catfish has a flat head and a wide mouth. It can grow to a very large size. The wels catfish can even come out of the water and grab birds to eat.

COMMON EUROPEAN ADDER

Length: 26 inches (66 centimeters)
Weight: 6 ounces (170 grams)
Habitat: forests and wetlands of northern and eastern Europe
Diet: birds, frogs, and small mammals

MEDITERRANEAN BLACK WIDOW SPIDER

Length: ½ inch (1.3 centimeters)
Habitat: grasslands of southern Europe
Diet: insects

The European adder (**ADD-er**), or viper, is the only venomous snake in England. Males fight each other by doing "the dance of the adder." The two snakes lift themselves straight up and begin to push into each other.

During the summer, people in Southern Europe know to watch out for the Mediterranean black widow spider. A single bite from this spider can be deadly.

NORTHERN LYNX

Length: 51 inches (130 centimeters),
including tail
Weight: 65 pounds (29 kilograms)
Habitat: mountains and forests of
northern and eastern Europe
Diet: small mammals, birds,
fish, deer, and sheep

The northern lynx (**LINKS**) lives in forests and mountains. It has thick fur to keep it warm in the winter. The fur on its ears helps them hear its prey. Lynx use their special coloring to hide. They can jump 6½ feet (2 meters) in the air to catch a bird.

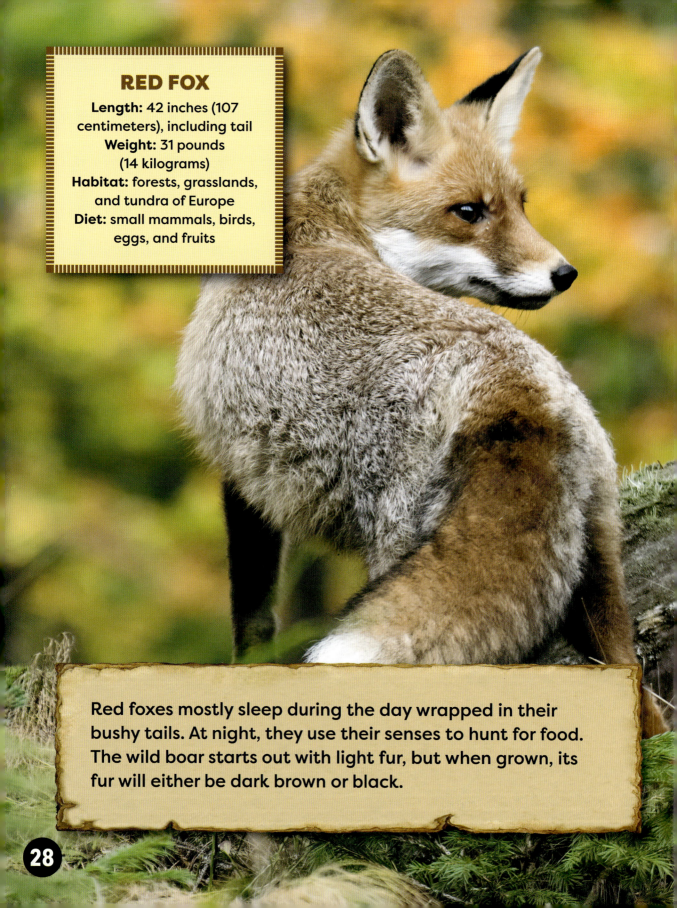

RED FOX

Length: 42 inches (107 centimeters), including tail
Weight: 31 pounds (14 kilograms)
Habitat: forests, grasslands, and tundra of Europe
Diet: small mammals, birds, eggs, and fruits

Red foxes mostly sleep during the day wrapped in their bushy tails. At night, they use their senses to hunt for food. The wild boar starts out with light fur, but when grown, its fur will either be dark brown or black.

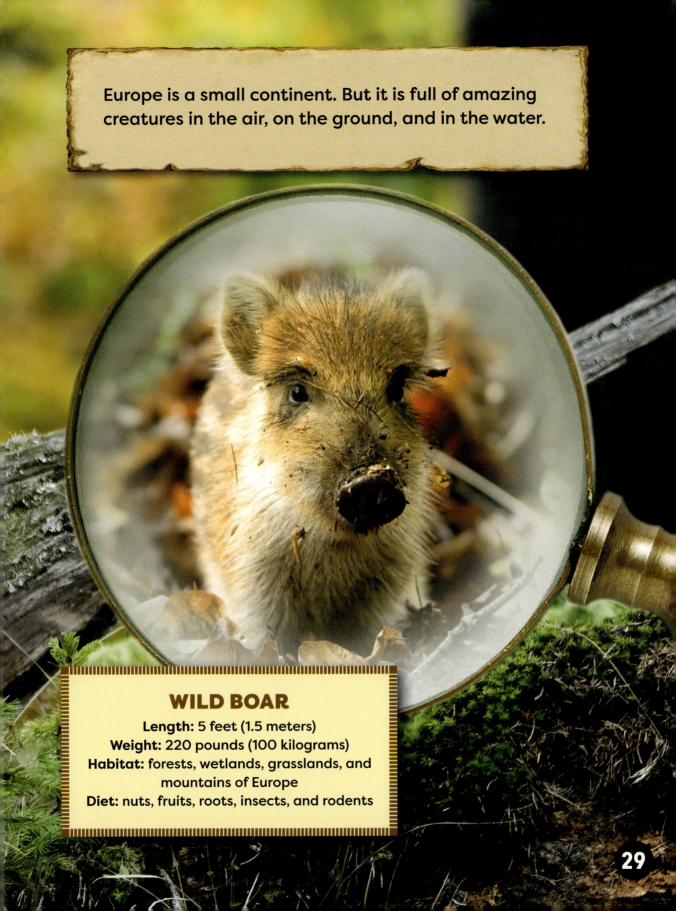

Europe is a small continent. But it is full of amazing creatures in the air, on the ground, and in the water.

WILD BOAR

Length: 5 feet (1.5 meters)
Weight: 220 pounds (100 kilograms)
Habitat: forests, wetlands, grasslands, and mountains of Europe
Diet: nuts, fruits, roots, insects, and rodents

FURTHER READING

Books

Allgor, Marie. *Endangered Animals of Europe.* Powerkids Press, 2011.

Jackson, Tom. *The Illustrated Encyclopedia of Animals of Africa, Britain and Europe.* Lorenz Books, 2008.

Sherwood, Sandra E. *Animals in Europe—Enjoy and Learn about Your World.* Amazon Digital Services, 2012.

Spilsbury, Richard. *Animals in Danger in Europe.* Heinemann, 2013.

Websites

Active Wild: European Animals List with Pictures & Facts
https://www.activewild.com/european-animals

Enchanted Learning: European Animals
http://www.enchantedlearning.com/coloring/europe.shtml

Ducksters: Europe Geography
https://www.ducksters.com/geography/europe.php

GLOSSARY

biome (BY-ohm)—Any major region that has a specific climate and supports specific animals and plants.

continent (KON-tih-nunt)—One of the seven great pieces of land on Earth.

Eurasian (yoor-A-shun)—Coming from both continents of Europe and Asia.

hibernate (HY-bur-nayt)—To sleep and stay inside during the winter months.

tundra (TON-druh)—A plain with very little plant life that has a permanently frozen layer below the surface.

venom (VEN-um)—Poison inserted into the body instead of eaten.

viper (VY-purr)—A type of dangerous snake.

PHOTO CREDITS

CHECK OUT THE OTHER BOOKS IN THE AWESOME ANIMALS SERIES

Awesome Animals of Africa
Awesome Animals of Antarctica
Awesome Animals of Asia
Awesome Animals of Australia
Awesome Animals of North America
Awesome Animals of South America

Paperback ISBN 979-8-89094-107-7
Hardcover ISBN 979-8-89094-108-4

Library of Congress Control Number: 2024932970

To learn more about the other great books from Fox Chapel Publishing, or to find a retailer near you, call toll-free 800-457-9112 or visit us at *www.FoxChapelPublishing.com*.

We are always looking for talented authors. To submit an idea, please send a brief inquiry to acquisitions@foxchapelpublishing.com.

Fox Chapel Publishing makes every effort to use environmentally friendly paper for printing.

Printed in Malaysia

NORTH POLE
ARCTIC OCEAN
GREENLAND
NORTH AMERICA
EUROPE
ASIA
PACIFIC OCEAN
ATLANTIC OCEAN
AFRICA
SOUTH AMERICA
INDIAN OCEAN
AUSTRALIA
PACIFIC OCEAN
SOUTH POLE
ANTARCTICA